Our Wonder-Filled World

by

Mary Tadokoro

Asahi Press

音声再生アプリ「リスニング・トレーナー」を使った音声ダウンロード

朝日出版社開発のアプリ、「リスニング・トレーナー（リストレ）」を使えば、教科書の音声をスマホ、タブレットに簡単にダウンロードできます。どうぞご活用ください。

◉ アプリ【リスニング・トレーナー】の使い方

《アプリのダウンロード》

App Store または Google Play から「リスニング・トレーナー」のアプリ（無料）をダウンロード

App Storeはこちら▶

Google Playはこちら▶

《アプリの使い方》

① アプリを開き「コンテンツを追加」をタップ
② 画面上部に【15701】を入力しDoneをタップ

音声ストリーミング配信 》》》

この教科書の音声は、右記ウェブサイトにて無料で配信しています。

https://text.asahipress.com/free/english/

Our Wonder-Filled World
Copyright © 2023 by Asahi Press

All rights reserved. No part of this book may be reproduced or transmitted in any form or by any means, electronic or mechanical, including photocopying, recording or by any information storage and retrieval system, without permission in writing from author and the publisher.

Photographs by iStockphoto and ac-illust
Illustrations by Yasuco Sudaka (Unit 3, 4, 8) and Maiko Suzuki (Unit 2)

ま え が き

　私たちの身近にある、普段はあまり気にかけない物や事象について、ふと「あれは何だろう、何故だろう？」と思うことはないでしょうか。本書はその謎や疑問に答えるべく編まれた読解中心の総合教材です。Pre-reading として、基礎知識の Fast Fact や「なぞなぞ」の質問に始まり、易しい英文で書かれた Reading Passage、Topic の追加を材料にした Listening、様々な Exercises、学んだことを話し合う Dialog で構成されています。

　基礎知識を紹介している Pre-reading の問題では、推測が必要です。文章のつながりに気をつけながら答えてみてください。講読中心の教材ですが、大いに声を出して勉強することをお勧めします。Passage と More on the Topic では、Vocabulary を見てから、本文にスラッシュ（／）を入れながら、文章を区切って、シャドウイング (shadowing) をして口を慣らしましょう。そして、また声を出しながら、区切りごとの英語を日本語に訳しながらペアワークなどして練習を重ねましょう。最後に全体を通して訳してから、本文の英語を再度読み上げましょう。知らない間にその英語が浸透していきます。

　英語の上達はもちろんですが、世の中の不思議に圧倒される 1 年になるように願っています。

2022 年 10 月

田所メアリー

Contents

Our Wonder-Filled World

Lesson

1

Why Is the Ocean Salty?

PRE-READING TASKS

Fast Fact

The saltiness of the ocean, on average, is 35 grams of salts per liter.

A 次の 1.～3.の文の空欄に入る適切なものを a.～c.から選び、文章を完成させましょう。

1. Salt water is a combination of fresh water and _____, called salts.
2. These salts contain not just sodium and chloride, like table salt, but _____ as well.
3. The saltiness of the world's oceans ranges from _____.

    a. calcium, magnesium, potassium, and other minerals

    b. 30 to 38 grams per liter

    c. minerals

B なぞなぞに挑戦してみましょう。

I am not salty, but over time I make the oceans salty. What am I?

● Take a guess: You are _____.

● Read the passage to find out the answer!

Vocabulary _____

saltiness: 塩味　　**on average:** 平均して　　**sodium:** ナトリウム　　**chloride:** 塩化物
range from A to B: ～は A から B までにわたる　　**potassium:** カリウム
over time: 時が経つにつれて

READING

The rivers that flow into the ocean are not salty. So why is the ocean salty? Scientists give two major reasons: the action of the earth's crust and the action of rain.

First, minerals enter the ocean through the earth's crust. For example,
5 fissures and underwater volcanoes bring up minerals from inside the earth.

Second, rain and wind break down rocks. The rain carries minerals from the rocks into rivers. Those rivers flow into the ocean. The sun evaporates water from the rivers and ocean, but the minerals stay in the water. The most common minerals in the ocean are chloride and sodium. They
10 make up 85 percent of the minerals in the ocean.

Marine plants and animals use some of the minerals. But the rest stay in the water or sink to the bottom of the ocean. Over millions of years, the water in the ocean has become more and more salty.

Vocabulary ————————

earth's crust: 地殻　　**fissure:** 亀裂　　**bring up:** 噴き上げる
break down: 壊す、分解する　　**flow into:** 〜に流れ込む　　**evaporate:** 蒸発する
make up: 構成する、占める

POST-READING TASKS

A **Check your answer.**

なぞなぞの答えを確認しましょう。

I am not salty, but I carry salts to the ocean. What am I?

ANSWER: You are a _____.

B **Complete the sentences.**

1.~5. の文の空欄に入る最も適切なものを a.~e.から選び、文章を完成させましょう

1. Scientists give two major reasons for _____.
2. Minerals are brought up from inside the earth _____.
3. Rocks are broken down _____.
4. The sun evaporates _____.
5. Sodium and chloride _____.

    a. water but not minerals

    b. the saltiness of the ocean

    c. make up 85 percent of the salts in the ocean

    d. by the wind and rain

    e. through fissures and underwater volcanoes

C **More on the Topic**

録音を聞いて、（　　　）を埋めましょう。

Some parts of the (　　　　) are (　　　　) salty than other parts. It's (　　　) salty near the (　　　　) of rivers. And it's less salty at the (　　　) and (　　　) poles when the polar (　　　　) melts. The Pacific is much (　　　) and (　　　　) salty than the Atlantic. Deep, cold water is also (　　　) salty. But, at (　　　　) grams of salt per liter, the (　　　　) area is the Mediterranean Sea. So (　　　) (　　　　) salt is there in the ocean? Scientists say, if all the (　　　　) in the (　　　　) was dried and spread on the earth's (　　　　), it would be about (　　　) (　　　　) deep. That is about (　　　　) the height of (　　　) (　　　　).

Vocabulary

pole: 極、極地   **the Pacific (Ocean):** 太平洋   **the Atlantic (Ocean):** 大西洋
deep: 深い、深さ   **the Mediterranean Sea:** 地中海   **height:** 高さ

D Answer the questions.

1.～5. の質問の答えを a.～f.から選んで、空欄に記入しましょう

_____ **1.** Where is the ocean less salty?
_____ **2.** Which is smaller and more salty, the Atlantic or the Pacific?
_____ **3.** Which is less salty, surface water or deep water?
_____ **4.** How much saltier is the Mediterranean Sea than the average?
_____ **5.** If all the salt in the ocean were spread on the surface of the Earth,
how much higher would it be?

    a. It would be about 150 meters higher.
    b. It's about 3 grams per liter saltier.
    c. The Atlantic.
    d. The Pacific.
    e. In areas where fresh water enters it.
    f. Water near the surface of the ocean is.

E What did you learn from the lesson?

録音を聴いて（　　）に単語をいれ、ペアになって会話を練習しましょう。

A: How did you enjoy the lesson?

B: Well, I found it (　　　　　). And you?

A: I found it (　　　　　). What did you find (　　　　　)?

B: Well, I discovered that water from rivers makes the ocean salty! What about you?

A: Yeah, I didn't know that some parts of the ocean are saltier than others.

Lesson 2 Water All Around Us

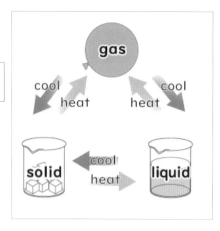

PRE-READING TASKS

Fast Fact

Water can be a gas, a liquid, or a solid.

A 次の 1.~3.の文の空欄に入る適切なものを a.~c.から選び、文章を完成させましょう。

1. Water in the air _____.
2. Water in lakes and the ocean _____.
3. Frozen water, such as ice and snow, _____.

    a. is a liquid.
    b. is a gas called vapor.
    c. is a solid.

B なぞなぞに挑戦してみましょう。

You cannot see me, but I hold more water than all the rivers in the world. What am I?

● Take a guess: You are the _____.

● Read the passage to find out the answer!

Vocabulary _____

(a) **gas:** 気体   (a) **liquid:** 液体   (a) **solid:** 個体   **vapor:** 蒸気   **hold:** ～が入っている
more A than B: B よりも A が多い

READING

Why does water form on a glass of ice water? The air by the glass cools down, and vapor in the air turns into water on the glass. This is called condensation. When you boil water, you can see it turn into vapor. This is called evaporation.

5   Condensation and evaporation are important processes in nature. For example, as the sun heats water on the Earth's surface, the water turns into vapor. Vapor is very light and rises into the sky. It gathers together in the form of clouds. As the vapor cools, it turns into water again and falls back to Earth as rain and snow.

10   There is always water vapor in the air, even in very dry areas. In fact, the air holds more fresh water than all the rivers of the world.

The process of condensation and evaporation is called the water cycle. At a global level, it is a balanced process. Every second, about 16 million tons of water evaporates from the Earth's surface. And, at the same time, 15 every second, the same amount falls back to the Earth's surface.

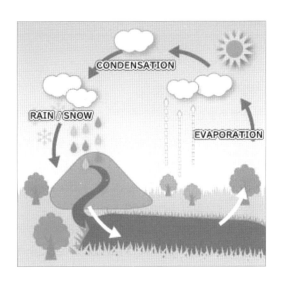

Vocabulary ————————

form: ～に生じる   **turn into/turn A into B:** ～に変わる/A が B に変わる
condensation: 凝縮   **evaporation:** 蒸発   **process:** 1 連の過程   **rise:** （高いところに）
上がる   **gather together:** 集まる   **in the form of:** ～の形で   **fall back to:** ～に（落
ちて）戻ってくる   **water cycle:** 水循環   **at a global level:** 世界的なレベルでは
evaporate: 蒸発する   **at the same time:** 同時に

POST-READING TASKS

A Check your answer.

なぞなぞの答えを確認しましょう。

You cannot see me, but I hold more water than all the rivers on earth. What am I?

ANSWER: You are the _____.

B Complete the sentences.

1.～4. の文の空欄に入る最も適切なものを a.～d.から選び、文章を完成させましょう

1. Water can be found in three forms, _____.
2. Condensation happens when _____.
3. Evaporation happens when _____.
4. The water cycle is _____.

    a. a very important natural process
    b. a gas turns into a liquid
    c. solid, liquid and gas
    d. a liquid turns into a gas

C More on the Topic

録音を聞いて、(　　) を埋めましょう。

By 2025, about (　　　　) of the people in the world will not have enough (　　　　). From 2016 to 2018, (　　　　) teams took part in an XPRIZE competition. They had to make (　　　　) liters of (　　　　) from the (　　　　) every (　　　　) hours for only (　　　　) cents a liter. Also they had to use renewable (　　　　). Only (　　　) (　　　　) succeeded. They made a (　　　　) called WeDew. It uses a (　　　　) called gasification. It superheats biomass and creates a (　　　) (　　　) inside the (　　　　). It also produces (　　　　) and biochar. WeDew is portable, so it can be used in disaster areas.

Vocabulary _____

take part in: 〜参加する　　**XPRIZE:**「X プライズ財団」1995 年に設立された非営利組織
make A for B: A を B（値段）で作る　　**renewable:** 再生可能　　**gasification:** ガス化、気（体）
化　　**superheat:** 過熱する　　**biomass:** 生物資源の総称、生物資源（bio）の量（mass）を表
す概念　　**biochar:** バイオ炭、生物由来の有機物（バイオマス）を炭化させたもの

D　Answer the questions.

1.〜6. の質問の答えを a.〜f.から選んで、空欄に記入しましょう

_____ **1.** How many people will lack water in 2025?
_____ **2.** How many teams competed in the contest?
_____ **3.** What did they have to do?
_____ **4.** How many teams were successful?
_____ **5.** What does gasification do to the biomass?
_____ **6.** What are the products of the WeDew machine?

    a. Create a lot of water from the air, fast and cheaply, using renewable energy.
    b. It superheats it and creates a water cycle.
    c. Water, electricity and biochar.
    d. More than half the people in the world.
    e. Almost a hundred.
    f. Only one was.

E　What did you learn from the lesson?

録音を聴いて（　　）に単語をいれ、ペアになって会話を練習しましょう。

A: How did you enjoy the lesson?

B: I found it (　　　　). And you?

A: I found it (　　　　). What did you find (　　　)?

B: Well, it's (　　　) that we can make water from air. What did you find (　　　)?

A: Well, Japan has so many disasters. I hope many WeDew machines will be used here.

Lesson 3 — Sky Art

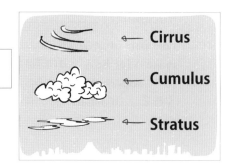

— Cirrus
— Cumulus
— Stratus

PRE-READING TASKS

Fast Fact

There are three main cloud types: cumulus, stratus and cirrus.

A　次の 1.～3.の文の空欄に入る適切なものを a.～c.から選び、文章を完成させましょう。

1. Often seen in summer, cumulus have a flat base ＿＿＿＿＿.
2. Stratus clouds are low-level clouds with a flat base, ＿＿＿＿＿.
3. Cirrus clouds are small, wispy clouds, ＿＿＿＿＿.

    a. and they often cover the entire sky
    b. and often look like they are dancing high in the sky
    c. and look like castles in the sky.

B　なぞなぞに挑戦してみましょう。

I seem to have no weight but am actually heavier than clouds that weigh many tons. What am I?

● Take a guess: You are ＿＿＿＿＿＿＿.

● Read the passage to find out the answer!

Vocabulary ＿＿＿＿＿＿

cumulus: 積雲　　**stratus:** 層雲　　**cirrus:** 巻雲　　**wispy:** かすかな

READING

Many people love watching clouds. They float far above us and change into different shapes. They seem to have no weight. If they were heavy, surely they would fall down on us!

But wait. Clouds form when water vapor in the air cools and water drop-
5 lets form. Water has weight, so clouds must have weight, too. But clouds can float in the air, so they must be lighter than the air below them!

The weight of a cloud depends on how much water is in it. In summer, we see a lot of cumulus clouds. The water in one cumulus weighs over 550 tons on average. That's the weight of about 100 elephants! And when a
10 cumulus grows into a huge, dark storm cloud, it can weigh over 3 million kilograms! Thank goodness they don't fall out of the sky and squish us!!

But, wait again. When the water droplets in a cloud get too heavy, they fall to the earth as rain. So, in a way, clouds do fall down on us!

Cumulus   100 elephants

Vocabulary ———————————

be lighter than: 〜より軽い   **A depends on B:** A は B によって決まる
grow into : 〜に育つ   **storm cloud:** 嵐雲   **thank goodness:** ありがたいことに
squish : つぶす   **in a way:** ある意味では

POST-READING TASKS

A Check your answer.

なぞなぞの答えを確認しましょう。

I seem to have no weight but am actually heavier than clouds that weigh many tons. What am I?

ANSWER: You are _____.

B Complete the sentences.

1.～5. の文の空欄に入る最も適切なものを a.～e.から選び、文章を完成させましょう

1. A lot of people enjoy _____.
2. Clouds float _____.
3. The weight of a cloud _____.
4. On average, a cumulus _____.
5. Dark storm clouds can weigh _____.

    a. because they are lighter than the air below them
    b. depends on how much water is in it
    c. six times more than cumulus clouds
    d. watching clouds
    e. weighs about 500,000 kilograms

C More on the Topic

録音を聞いて、（　　）を埋めましょう。

Why are beautiful sunrises and sunsets (　　　　) and (　　　　)? And, for that matter, why is the (　　　) (　　　　)? As the sun rises and sets, its light rays hit many small particles including dust, oxygen and nitrogen, and (　　　). The light rays scatter in various directions. From where we look, colors with (　　　　) wavelengths, like (　　　　) and violet, disappear. But we can still see colors with (　　　　) wavelengths, like the (　　　) and (　　　　). When the (　　　) is higher in the sky, the angle changes. Then the colors with (　　　) wavelengths are scattered, and we see only the (　　　　) wavelength, (　　　　). And that is why the (　　　) is (　　　　)!

Vocabulary

for that matter: そういえば **light rays:** 光線 **hit:** 当たる
particles: 粒子 **nitrogen:** 窒素 **scatter:** 散らばる **wavelength:** 波長

D Answer the questions.

1.～5. の質問の答えを a.～e.から選んで、空欄に記入しましょう

_____ **1.** What do the rays from the sun hit?
_____ **2.** What happens when the rays hit them?
_____ **3.** At sunrise or sunset, what happens to the short wavelengths?
_____ **4.** What colors have long wavelengths?
_____ **5.** What colors remain during the day?

   a. The rays scatter in many directions.
   b. Vivid colors like orange and red.
   c. Various tiny particles in the air.
   d. They disappear from our view.
   e. The ones with short wavelengths.

E What did you learn from the lesson?

録音を聴いて （   ） に単語をいれ、ペアになって会話を練習しましょう。

A: How did you enjoy the lesson?

B: Well, I found it (   ). And you?

A: I found it (   ). What did you find most (   )?

B: Well, I never stopped to think about how much a cloud weighs! I was surprised that they weigh so much! What about you?

A: Well, now I know why the sky is blue and why sunrises and sunsets are orange and red.

Lesson
4
The Illusion of a Rainbow

PRE-READING TASKS

Fast Fact

To create a rainbow, sunlight must hit a raindrop at 40 to 42 degrees, opposite to where you are.

A 次の 1.～3.の文の空欄に入る適切なものを a.～c.から選び、文章を完成させましょう。

1. Each raindrop is like a mirror, _____.
2. It is also like a prism, _____.
3. The bending of light is called refraction, _____.

    a. because sunlight bends as it goes in and out of it.
    b. because the light bounces off its back surface.
    c. and the bouncing back of light is called reflection.

B なぞなぞに挑戦してみましょう。

I am a rainbow. When you see me from below, I am an arch. What shape am I when you see me from above?

● Take a guess: You are a _____.

● Read the passage to find the answer!

Vocabulary _____

hit A at B degrees: A を B 角度で当てる   **opposite to:** ～の反対   **refraction:** 屈折
go in and out of: ～に入ったり出たり   **bounce off:** 跳ね返る   **bouncing back:** 跳ね返
り   **reflection:** 反射

READING

14

Rainbows are always a treat to see. Most people around the world believe they bring good luck. The Irish say there is a pot of gold at the end of a rainbow, and some people have even tried to find it.

But rainbows are optical phenomena. They have no actual physical
5 form. In order to see one, you must be at a certain angle from the sun. When you move, the rainbow always moves, too. So you will never find the end. In fact, if you see a rainbow from an airplane, the rainbow will be a circle, not an arch!

15

Sunlight must hit a raindrop at 40 to 42 degrees in order to create a
10 rainbow. That is why we usually see them in the morning or the later afternoon. A double rainbow occurs when light is reflected twice in each raindrop. The next time you see one, notice that the colors are reversed!

Most rainbows usually last for just a few minutes. But in 2017, in the mountains in Taipei, a rainbow lasted for almost nine hours from early
15 morning to late afternoon.

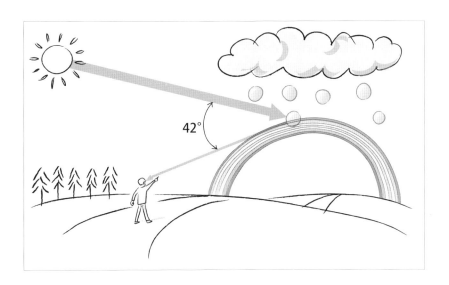

Vocabulary —————————

a treat to see: 見るのに楽しい   **at the end of:** ～の先   **optical phenomenon:** 光学現象
physical form: 物理的な形   **be at a certain angle from:** ～から一定の角度にいる
notice that: ～に注目する   **be reversed:** 反対になっている   **last for (time):** （時間が）続く

POST-READING TASKS

A **Check your answer.**

なぞなぞの答えを確認しましょう。

I am a rainbow. When you see me from below, I am an arch. What shape am I when you see me from above?

ANSWER: You are a _____.

B **Complete the sentences.**

1.~5. の文の空欄に入る最も適切なものを a.~e.から選び、文章を完成させましょう

1. People all around the world _____.
2. You will never find the end of a rainbow _____.
3. Rainbows usually don't occur around noon _____.
4. When light is reflected twice in the raindrops _____.
5. The time record for a rainbow _____.

    a. because it moves as you move

    b. a double rainbow can be seen

    c. is about nine hours

    d. believe that rainbows are a sign of good luck

    e. because the sun is too high in the sky

C **More on the Topic**

録音を聞いて、（　　）を埋めましょう。

16

In ancient Greek mythology, the gods and goddesses (　　　　　) on Mt. Olympus, above the (　　　　). People believed (　　　　) were their path down to Earth. The goddess Iris represented the (　　　　　). She would come down to Earth and scoop up (　　　　) with her pitcher. Then she would pour it from the (　　　　) to form the (　　　　). Many ancient cultures believed that (　　　　) were living creatures. The ancient Chinese thought it was a dragon or giant serpent. It (　　　　) (　　　　) from the (　　　　) after a rain. The ancient Japanese, like the Greeks, thought it was a (　　　　) for the gods. But they thought that rainbows brought (　　　　) luck, not (　　　　) luck.

Vocabulary ────────────

mythology : 神話　　　**Mt. Olympus:** オリンポス山　　　**path down to:** 〜に降りてくる道
represent : 象徴する　　　**scoop up:** すくいあげる　　　**pitcher:** 水差し
living creature: 生き物　　　**serpent:** 蛇

D Answer the questions.

1.〜6. の質問の答えを a.〜f.から選んで、空欄に記入しましょう

_____ **1.** Where did the Greek gods and goddesses live?
_____ **2.** What did the ancient Greeks and Japanese believe rainbows were?
_____ **3.** Which goddess represented the rainbow?
_____ **4.** What did she do when she came down to Earth?
_____ **5.** What did the ancient Chinese believe rainbows were?
_____ **6.** What did the ancient Japanese believe about rainbows?

a. Iris did.
b. That they were the gods′ paths to Earth.
c. Living creatures.
d. They were unlucky.
e. On Mt. Olympus.
f. She scooped up water to pour from the clouds.

E What did you learn from the lesson?

録音を聴いて（　　）に単語をいれ、ペアになって会話を練習しましょう。

A: How did you enjoy the lesson?

B: Well, I found it a bit (　　　　　). And you?

A: I found it (　　　　). What did you find (　　　　)?

B: Well, I love rainbows, but the way they are made is a bit hard to under-
stand. What did you find (　　　　)?

A: I found the legends about rainbows to be quite (　　　　　).

Lesson 5

Lightning, Nature's Fireworks

PRE-READING TASKS

Fast Fact

Scientists estimate lightning strikes somewhere on Earth over 100 times per second.

A 次の 1.～4.の文の空欄に入る適切なものを a.～d.から選び、文章を完成させましょう。

1. All things _____.
2. Neutrons and protons make up the nucleus, _____.
3. Protons have a positive electric charge, _____.
4. Opposite charges attract each other, _____.

 a. are made up of atoms
 b. and similar charges repel each other
 c. and electrons have a negative electric charge
 d. and electrons move around the nucleus

B なぞなぞに挑戦してみましょう。

I make your hair stand on end, and I cause lightning, too. What am I?

● Take a guess: You are _____.

● Read the passage to find out the answer!

Vocabulary _____

lightning: 稲光　　**fireworks:** 花火　　**neutron:** 中性子　　**proton:** 陽子　　**nucleus:** 核　**charge:** 電荷　　**attract each other:** 引き合う　　**repel:** 反発する　　**stand on end:** 逆立てる　　**cause:** 引き起こす

READING

Has your hair ever stood on end when you brushed it? Why does this happen? And how is it related to lightning? Both are related to static electricity. First, recall that electrons have a negative charge. Also recall that opposite charges attract each other.

5　Static electricity is a charge. It builds up on something when its atoms move. Then, when that thing comes in contact with another thing, the electrons on its surface transfer to the other surface. For example, if your hair stands on end when you brush it, the electrons from your hairbrush have transferred to your hair. Sometimes you may feel a shock when they trans-
10 fer, for example, when you touch a car or a doorknob.

On a much larger scale, lightning is also caused by static electricity. Inside a storm cloud, water and ice move around. That creates static electricity. The bottom part of a storm cloud becomes negatively charged. The top part becomes positively charged. The charges attract each other, so a lot
15 of lightning happens inside clouds.

But during a storm, the earth also becomes positively charged. When the cloud's negative charge becomes very strong, it is attracted to the earth's positive charge. That's when we can see nature's amazing fireworks display.

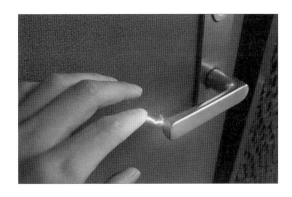

Vocabulary ───────────

relate to: 〜と関係がある　　**static electricity:** 静電気　　**recall that:** 〜を思い出す
build up ~: 〜が増大する　　**come in contact with:** 〜と接触する
transfer from A to B: A から B へ移動する　　**negatively:** （電荷が）マイナスに
positively: （電荷が）プラスに　　**fireworks display:** 花火大会

POST-READING TASKS

A **Check your answer.**

なぞなぞの答えを確認しましょう。

I make people's hair stand on end, and I cause lightning, too. What am I?

ANSWER: You are _____.

B **Complete the sentences.**

1.～5. の文の空欄に入る最も適切なものを a.～e.から選び、文章を完成させましょう

1. Static electricity is responsible for _____.
2. A negative charge and a positive charge _____.
3. When our hair stands on end, _____.
4. Lightning happens inside clouds _____.
5. A negative lightning strike occurs _____.

    a. because the top and bottom have opposite charges
    b. our hair standing on end, electric shocks, and lightning
    c. when the cloud's negative charge is attracted to the earth's positive charge
    d. each hair has a negative charge, so they all repel each other
    e. attract each other

C **More on the Topic**

録音を聞いて、（　　）を埋めましょう。

Here are a few more interesting facts about lightning. Lightning bolts look (　　　　), but they are actually only about the width of your (　　　　). The (　　　　) around a lightning bolt is (　　　　) times hotter than the (　　　　)! Thunder is the (　　　　) of the (　　　　) suddenly expanding from the (　　　　). And finally, did you know that the lightning we see is actually traveling (　　　　) not (　　　　)?! An invisible impulse is sent (　　　　) from the (　　　　). Just as it gets near the (　　　　), a positive charge reaches (　　　　) to meet it. This travels up at almost (　　　　) million km/hr! But still, I wonder why we see the lightning (　　　　) (　　　　).

Vocabulary

width: 幅　　**travel up/down:** 上昇する／下降する　　**impulse:** 衝撃
wonder why: なぜだろうと思う

D Answer the questions.

1.～6. の質問の答えを a.～g. から選んで、空欄に記入しましょう

_____ **1.** What is the diameter of a lightning bolt?
_____ **2.** How hot is the air around a bolt?
_____ **3.** Why does thunder occur?
_____ **4.** What direction does a lightning bolt actually travel?
_____ **5.** What is sent down from the cloud?
_____ **6.** How fast does the positive charge from the earth travel up?

    a. At about 100 million km/hr.
    b. It's caused by the air expanding as it gets hot.
    c. Several times hotter than the sun.
    d. It travels up.
    e. It travels down.
    f. About 2 centimeters wide.
    g. An impulse.

E What did you learn from the lesson?

録音を聴いて（　　）に単語をいれ、ペアになって会話を練習しましょう。

A: How did you enjoy the lesson?

B: Well, I found it (　　　　). And you?

A: I found it (　　　　). What did you find (　　　　)?

B: Well, I didn't know static electricity was the cause of lightning. What did you find (　　　　)?

A: Well, I was surprised to learn that lightning is actually traveling up, not down.

Lesson
6   Firefly Delight

PRE-READING TASKS

Fast Fact

There are 2,000 species of fireflies throughout the world.

A 次の 1.〜3.の文の空欄に入る適切なものを a.〜c.から選び、文章を完成させましょう。

1. Fireflies are beetles, which have hard forewings _____.
2. Only 10 species are aquatic, _____.
3. The rest are terrestrial, _____.

>   **a.** that is, the larvae grow on land
>   **b.** that is, the larvae grow in water
>   **c.** that meet at the back in a straight line

B なぞなぞに挑戦してみましょう。

I am a firefly that is native to Japan. I am rather large and emit a slow, bright light. What kind of firefly am I?

● Take a guess: You are a _____.

● Read the passage to find out the answer!

Vocabulary _____

beetle: 甲虫類   **forewing:**（昆虫の）前翅   **aquatic:** 水生の   **terrestrial:** 地上の
larvae: 幼虫   **in a straight line:** 一直線に   **be native to:** 〜の原産   **emit:** 放つ

READING

22

Fireflies are loved all over the world, especially here in Japan. Over 40 species can be found here. The best known are the Genji and the Heike fireflies. In many places, they can be seen flying together. One legend is that their flashing light reminded people of the last Genpei battle of 1185.
5 They said the souls of the Genji and Heike soldiers were still battling in death. But there are other theories about how these fireflies got their names, too.

23

The adult Genji firefly is about 1.5 to 2 cm long. Its light is big, bright and flashes slowly. The Heike firefly is about half that size. Its light is very
10 small and flashes rapidly. Both are aquatic. They do not move far. Interestingly, the light of the Genji firefly is different in Eastern and Western Japan. In Eastern Japan, it flashes slower, once every four seconds, but in Western Japan it flashes faster, once every two seconds.

Most fireflies live for about a year. They spend about a month as eggs,
15 a year as larvae, two weeks as pupae, and a few weeks as an adult firefly. Not all adult fireflies emit light to attract a mate, but all species glow as eggs, larvae and pupae. The light seems to warn predators that they do not taste good.

Vocabulary _____

remind A of B: A に B を思い起こさせる　　**battle:** 闘う　　**in death:** 死んでいても
theory: 説　　**once every ~ seconds :** 〜秒に 1 回　　**pupae:** サナギ
not all A do B: 全部の A が B をするわけではない　　**attract:** 誘う、引き付ける
seem to do: 〜しているようだ　　**predator:** 捕食者

POST-READING TASKS

A **Check your answer.**

なぞなぞの答えを確認しましょう。

I am a firefly that is native to Japan. I am rather large and emit a slow, bright light. What kind of firefly am I?

ANSWER: You are a _____.

B **Complete the sentences.**

1.~5. の文の空欄に入る最も適切なものを a.~e.から選び、文章を完成させましょう

1. Out of 2,000 firefly species, _____.
2. There is more than one story about _____.
3. The Genji firefly is _____.
4. The larvae of both the Genji and Heikei fireflies _____.
5. Some but not all adult fireflies _____.

    a. emit light to attract a mate
    b. how the Genji and Heikei fireflies got their names
    c. almost twice as big as the Heikei firefly
    d. live in the water
    e. over 40 can be found in Japan

C **More on the Topic**

録音を聞いて、（　　）を埋めましょう。

(　　　　) have been very interested in the (　　　　) that (　　　) emit. They found that a chemical reaction between the enzyme luciferase and lucifern produces the (　　　　). Only (　　　　), no (　　　), is produced. Compare that to incandescent light bulbs. They give off (　　　) percent (　　　) and only (　　　) percent (　　　)! Various (　　　) uses for luciferase have been developed. For example, it helps (　　　) to find blood clots and tuberculosis virus cells. It is also used to monitor the level of hydrogen peroxide, which may play a role in (　　　　) and diabetes.

Vocabulary _____

chemical reaction: 化学反応　　　**enzyme:** 酵素、エンザイム　　　**luciferase:** ルシフェラーゼ

lucifern : ルシファーン　　　**incandescent light bulb:** 白熱電球　　　**give off:** 放つ

blood clot : 血栓　　　**tuberculosis:** 結核　　　**hydrogen peroxide:** 過酸化水素

play a role in : ～で役割を果たす　　　**diabetes:** 糖尿病

D　**Answer the questions.**

1.～6. の質問の答えを a.～f.から選んで、空欄に記入しましょう

_____ **1.** What are scientists interested in?
_____ **2.** How is a fireflies' light produced?
_____ **3.** How efficient is this process?
_____ **4.** What does it not produce?
_____ **5.** How energy efficient are incandescent light bulbs?
_____ **6.** What does luciferase help doctors do?

   a. By a chemical reaction.
   b. Heat.
   c. 10 percent.
   d. How fireflies emit light.
   e. 100 percent.
   f. Find blood clots and tuberculosis cells.

E　**What did you learn from the lesson?**

録音を聴いて (　　) に単語をいれ、ペアになって会話を練習しましょう。

A: How did you enjoy the lesson?

B: Well, I found it (　　　　　). And you?

A: I found it (　　　　　). What did you find (　　　　　)?

B: Well, I didn't know much about fireflies, so I learned a lot. What did
   you find (　　　　)?

A: Well, I found the legend of Genji and Heike spirits fighting even in
   death very (　　　　). I hope to see them flying together sometime.

Lesson

7 What Is in This Flower's Name?

PRE-READING TASKS

Fast Fact

A plant or animal may have many common names, but only one scientific name.

A 次の 1.〜3.の文の空欄に入る適切なものを a.〜c.から選び、文章を完成させましょう。

1. In the 1750s, a Swedish scientist named Carl Linnaeus ＿＿＿＿＿＿.
2. A family name, called the genus, comes first, ＿＿＿＿＿＿.
3. Latin is used, ＿＿＿＿＿＿.

    a. developed a two-name system for plants and animals

    b. and that name is the same all over the world

    c. followed by the family member's name, called the species

B なぞなぞに挑戦してみましょう。

My flower looks like the sun, my seed ball looks like the moon, and my seeds look like stars as they fly away. What am I?

● Take a guess: You are a ＿＿＿＿＿＿＿＿.

● Read the passage to find out the answer!

Vocabulary ＿＿＿＿＿＿＿＿

common name: 通称　　scientific name: 学名　　genus: 属
(be) followed by: 〜に続く　　seed ball: 種球　　fly away : 飛び去る

READING

Humans love to give names to things, and that includes plants and flowers. Both scientific and common names often describe a special characteristic. For example, its color or shape, or where it grows. Some names even contain a hidden story.

5   The common name of one flower has been translated into many languages, even Japanese. Here they are called *wasurenagusa*. They are called forget-me-nots in English. Do you know the story behind the name of these tiny blue flowers?

   In a legend from Germany, two lovers were walking along the River Danube. 10 They saw some lovely little blue flowers growing by the river. The man climbed down and picked some. But, as he was coming back, he was carried away by the river. He threw the flowers to his love and shouted, "Don't forget me!" She wore these flowers in her hair until she died. And that is how they got the name "forget-me-not."

15   Another flower loved by children all around the world is the dandelion. Its English name makes children think of sunny yellow lions. The flower is bright yellow, and its name sounds like "dandy lion." But its name actually comes from the French *dent de lion* and means "lion's tooth." That describes the shape of the leaves, not the flower!

Vocabulary _____

describe: 表す   **hidden:** 隠された   **the River Danube:** ドナウ川
grow: 成長する   **climb down:** 降りる   **be carried away by:** 〜に流される
dandelion: タンポポ   **sound like:** 〜のように聞こえる

POST-READING TASKS

A **Check your answer.**

なぞなぞの答えを確認しましょう。

My flower looks like the sun, my seed ball looks like the moon, and my seeds look like stars as they fly away. What am I?

ANSWER: You are a _____.

B **Complete the sentences.**

1.～5. の文の空欄に入る最も適切なものを a.～e. から選び、文章を完成させましょう

1. A "common name" is _____.
2. They often describe the thing's _____.
3. Forget-me-nots got _____.
4. "Forget me not" is a formal way of saying _____.
5. Dandelions actually got their name _____.

    a. their name from a sad love story
    b. color or shape
    c. "Don't forget me"
    d. from the shape of their leaves
    e. a name that regular people give to things

C **More on the Topic**

録音を聞いて、(　　　) を埋めましょう。

One delightful plant is called *ojigisou* in Japanese. When you (　　　　　) them, they look as if they are (　　　　　), don't they? What is its name in English? First, its (　　　　) name is *Mimosa Pudica*. In Latin, *pudica* means to shrink or pretend to be (　　　　). (　　　　　) people often lower their (　　　　) and (　　　　), and their (　　　　) folds down and in. That is the image behind its (　　　　) name. Its (　　　　) names include sensitive plant and (　　　) plant. Another is (　　　)-me-not. Actually, the (　　　) fold up in order to protect themselves. This is stressful and takes a lot of (　　　). So perhaps they really are saying, "Don't (　　　) me!!!"

Vocabulary _____

look as if: まるで〜のように見える　　　**shrink:** 縮こまる　　　**pretend to be:** 〜のふりをする
lower (v): 下げる　　　**fold down and in:** 縮める

D　Answer the questions.

1.〜6. の質問の答えを a.〜f.から選んで、空欄に記入しましょう

_____ **1.** What do the leaves of the *Mimosa Pudica* do when you touch them?
_____ **2.** What does *Pudica* mean?
_____ **3.** How does a person act when they are shy?
_____ **4.** What are a couple of its common English names?
_____ **5.** Why do the leaves react when touched?
_____ **6.** Why might the plant be saying, Don't touch me!?

    a. They lower their head and bring their shoulders forward.
    b. Because it is stressful and takes a lot of energy.
    c. Shy plant and touch-me-not.
    d. They fold up.
    e. In order to protect themselves.
    f. It means to get smaller.

E　What did you learn from the lesson?

録音を聴いて （　　） に単語をいれ、ペアになって会話を練習しましょう。

A: How did you enjoy the lesson?

B: Well, I loved it, but I found it a bit (　　　　　). And you?

A: I found it (　　　　). What did you find (　　　　)?

B: Oh, the story behind the forget-me-nots was so (　　　　). What did
you find (　　　)?

A: The stories behind the names of plants. I want to read more.

Lesson

8

From 4 to over 400, Colors in Japan

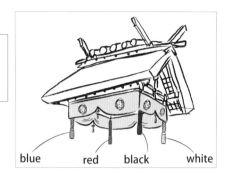

blue   red   black   white

PRE-READING TASKS

Fast Fact

Japan has a special relationship with four colors: black, red, blue and white.

A 次の 1.～3.の文の空欄に入る適切なものを a.～c.から選び、文章を完成させましょう。

1. Only these four colors can _____.
2. They are the only colors _____.
3. Black, red, and white were used in religious life, _____.

    a. take the prefix "真 (ma-)," meaning pure

    b. while blue was used in daily life

    c. that can take the adjective suffix "い (-i)"

B なぞなぞに挑戦してみましょう。

You can see me at a sumo tournament over the sumo ring. I represent the four directions. What am I?

● Take a guess: You are the _____.

● Read the passage to find out the answer!

Vocabulary _____

have a relationship with : ～と関係を持っている   **prefix:** 接頭辞   **suffix:** 接尾辞

READING

If you look at a color guide of Japanese colors, you will find over 400 distinct colors. The Japanese culture indeed has a long, unique relationship with colors. But did you know that in ancient Japan, there were only four names for colors?! According to Miura Sukeyuki, only 黒 (*kuro*, black), 赤 (*aka*, red), 青 (*ao*, blue) and 白 (*shiro*, white) were mentioned in the Kojiki and Nihon Shoki.

The 青 (*ao*) ranged from blue to green. This usage can still be seen in modern-day Japanese. For example, the word for a green traffic light is *ao shingo* (青信号), not *midori shingo* (緑信号). This, of course, confuses many foreigners.

The system originally came from ancient China. According to Hayashi Osamu, the colors were used in relation to the four directions. Black was north, which is dark (暗し or 玄). Red was south, which was light (明かし or 朱). Blue was east, which was vague (あわし). White was west, which was clear (しるし). They also referred to the seasons. 玄冬 means dark winter. 青春 means blue spring. 朱夏 means red summer. 白秋 means white autumn.

You can still see this system in use at a sumo tournament. Look at the four huge tassels hanging above the sumo ring. You will see black, red, blue and white, representing the four directions.

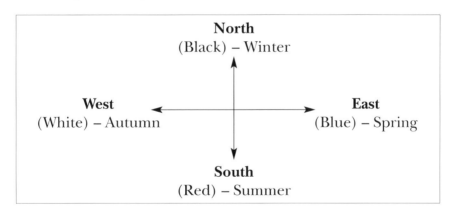

Vocabulary ───────────

color guide: 色彩図鑑 **distinct:** 独自の **according to:** 〜によって
Miura Sukeyuki: 三浦佑之 **Kojiki:** 古事記 **Nihon Shoki:** 日本書紀
be mentioned in: 〜に載っている **confuse:** 混乱させる **Hayashi Osamu:** 林修
vague (あわし)**:** 曖昧な **clear** (しるし)**:** 澄んでいる **refer to:** 〜を参照する
tassel: 飾り房

POST-READING TASKS

A Check your answer.

なぞなぞの答えを確認しましょう。

You can see me at a sumo tournament over the sumo ring. I represent the four directions. What am I?

ANSWER: You are the _____.

B Complete the sentences.

1.～5. の文の空欄に入る最も適切なものを a.～e.から選び、文章を完成させましょう

1. The names of only four colors _____.
2. The Japanese color 青 (*ao*) _____.
3. Black, red, blue and white were used _____.
4. They also represented _____.
5. The white tassel above the sumo dojo _____.

    a. to represent the four directions
    b. ranges from blue to green
    c. represents west
    d. the four seasons
    e. appear in the Kojiki and Nihon Shoki

C More on the Topic

録音を聞いて、( ) を埋めましょう。

32

The ancient ( ) concept of five elements also influenced the ( ) use of ( ). The universe was created of five elements: ( ), ( ), ( ), ( ) and ( ). Their corresponding colors were ( ), ( ), ( ), ( ) and ( ). In the 6th century, Shotoku Taishi created the Twelve Level Cap and Rank System. It was based on those five colors plus ( ). Each color had a deep version and a light version. The highest was deep ( ). People could not wear any color ( ) their ( ). But Japan's natural environment allowed many different ( ) to be created. And people enjoyed wearing many variations of the ( ) of their ( ).

Vocabulary

concept of five elements: 五行思想　　corresponding: 対応する　　Shotoku Taishi: 聖徳太子　　Twelve Level Cap and Rank System: 冠位十二階　　deep: 濃い　　light: 明るい　variation: 変化

D Answer the questions.

1.～6. の質問の答えを a.～f.から選んで、空欄に記入しましょう

_____ 1. What did the ancient Chinese believe about wood, fire, earth, metal and water?

_____ 2. What color does "earth" correspond to?

_____ 3. What color did Shotoku Taishi add to the five element colors?

_____ 4. Who could wear it?

_____ 5. What did a color tell you about a person?

_____ 6. How did people enjoy the colors of their rank?

    a. They made many variations of them.

    b. You could know their rank.

    c. Yellow.

    d. Purple.

    e. They made up the universe.

    f. Only people of the highest rank.

E What did you learn from the lesson?

録音を聴いて（　　）に単語をいれ、ペアになって会話を練習しましょう。

A: How did you enjoy the lesson?

B: Well, I found it (　　　　). And you?

A: I found it (　　　　). What did you find (　　　　)?

B: Well, here I live in Japan, but I never knew that ancient Japanese used only four colors. What did you find (　　　　)?

A: Well, I cannot imagine being told what color to wear! I'm glad we can wear any color we want now.

Lesson

9 The Soil under Our Feet

PRE-READING TASKS

Fast Fact

Soil contains 45% dirt, 25% water, 25% air and 5% organic matter.

A 次の 1.～3.の文の空欄に入る適切なものを a.～c.から選び、文章を完成させましょう。

1. Dirt is rock that has broken down, and ＿＿＿＿＿＿.
2. Organic, or living, matter ＿＿＿＿＿＿.
3. There are more organisms in 1 tablespoon of soil ＿＿＿＿＿＿.

   a. includes plant material, as well as worms, insects, fungi and bacteria
   b. than there are people on Earth
   c. it contains minerals like iron and magnesium

B なぞなぞに挑戦してみましょう。

I am called the only absolutely necessary industry. What am I?

● Take a guess: You are ＿＿＿＿＿＿＿＿.

● Read the passage to find out the answer!

Vocabulary ＿＿＿＿＿＿

dirt: 泥　　**organic matter:** 有機物　　**organism:** 生物、生命体　　**fungi:** 菌類

READING

Take a look at the ground. That brown stuff, called earth or soil, is the foundation of all life on Earth. Yes, even yours.

What does soil do for us? It is home to plants and trees. They provide us with food, shade and building materials. We use soil to make
5 bricks and concrete for buildings and roads. It produces the fossil fuels we use, as well. Healthy soil is a natural water filtration system. It helps to prevent both drought and flooding. Over 95% of all food production relies on soil. In fact, agriculture is called the only essential industry.

10 Soil may look dead, but healthy soil is actually teeming with life. One gram is home to 75,000 species of bacteria, 25,000 species of fungi, 1000 species of protozoa, and hundreds of species of nematodes. We still do not have names for over 99% of them. We know almost nothing about their activities and their complex transportation and communi-
15 cation networks.

But soil can die, too. How? Through poor agricultural practices, such as clearing, tilling and overuse. Chemical fertilizers disrupt the balance of the soil's ecosystem. Synthetic pesticides kill not only the pests but the living organisms in the soil as well. How healthy do you
20 think our soils are?

Vocabulary ――――――

take a look at: 〜を見てみよう   **be home to:** 〜の住処   **provide A with B:** A に B を提供する   **fossil fuel:** 化石燃料   **filtration system:** ろ過装置   **drought:** 干ばつ
flooding : 洪水   **rely on:** 〜に依存している   **teem with:** 〜で溢れている
protozoa: 原生動物   **nematode:** 線虫   **tilling:** 耕作   **overuse:** 過度の使用
fertilizer: 肥   **disrupt:** 崩す、妨害する   **synthetic pesticides:** 合成農薬

POST-READING TASKS

A **Check your answer.**

なぞなぞの答えを確認しましょう。

I am called the only absolutely necessary industry. What am I?

ANSWER: You are _____.

B **Complete the sentences.**

1.〜5. の文の空欄に入る最も適切なものを a.〜e.から選び、文章を完成させましょう

1. If there were no soil, _____.
2. We rely on soil for our _____.
3. Healthy soil can hold a lot of water, _____.
4. We know very little about _____.
5. It is possible _____.

    a. food, buildings, roads, and energy

    b. to kill the soil

    c. and it filters it as well

    d. there would be no life on Earth

    e. the organisms that live in the soil

C **More on the Topic**

録音を聞いて、（　　　）を埋めましょう。

36

The Earth's (　　　　) systems create no waste. Instead, they regenerate again and again. (　　　　) systems take from the Earth, but rarely (　　　) (　　　　). Not only that, they often poison and (　　　　) it! Modern agricultural practices such as (　　　　) and the use of synthetic pesticides and fertilizers have (　　　) the ecosystems of farm (　　　), (　　　) and even parts of the (　　　　). These practices are making people (　　　) as well. To survive and thrive, we must (　　　) and (　　　) Earth's (　　　) systems, especially the (　　　　) ecosystem. We need an agricultural system that renews the (　　　) again and again.

Vocabulary _____

waste: 廃棄物　　**regenerate:** 再生する　　**rarely:** めったに　　**poison (v):** 汚染する
thrive: 繁栄する

D Answer the questions.

1.～5. の質問の答えを a.～e. から選んで、空欄に記入しましょう

_____ **1.** What don't Earth's natural systems create?
_____ **2.** How are natural and manmade systems different?
_____ **3.** What have modern agricultural practices done?
_____ **4.** How do modern agricultural practices affect people?
_____ **5.** What kind of agricultural system is needed?

    a. They make them ill.
    b. They have killed the ecosystems in land, rivers and even parts of the ocean.
    c. They don't create waste.
    d. We need to create a regenerative agricultural system.
    e. Natural systems renew themselves while manmade ones destroy themselves.

E What did you learn from the lesson?

録音を聴いて（　　）に単語をいれ、ペアになって会話を練習しましょう。

A: How did you enjoy the lesson?

B: Well, I found it (　　　　). And you?

A: I found it (　　　　). What did you find (　　　　)?

B: Well, it's the first time I realized that natural systems don't create waste. What did you find (　　　　)?

A: Well, so much of the ecosystem has been destroyed. I wonder what we can do.

Lesson 10

Cacao, Food of the Gods

PRE-READING TASKS

Fast Fact

Chocolate is made from the seeds in the fruit of the cacao tree.

A 次の 1.～4.の文の空欄に入る適切なものを a.～d.から選び、文章を完成させましょう。

1. Most cacao trees grow _____, called cacao pods, each year.
2. Each pod holds _____, called cacao beans.
3. To produce 1 kilogram of chocolate _____ are needed.
4. On average, each tree produces only _____ of chocolate a year.

    a. 1 to 1.5 kilograms
    b. about 40 seeds
    c. over 800 cacao beans
    d. 30 to 60 fruits

B なぞなぞに挑戦してみましょう。

Even though chocolate has a long history, I wasn't invented until the early 1800s. What am I?

● Take a guess: You are _____.

● Read the passage to find out the answer!

Vocabulary _____

not ~ until : ～して初めて   **be invented:** 発明される   **early 1800s:** 1800 年代初頭

READING

A chocolate bar now sells for a hundred yen or so. But just 500 years ago, the Aztecs valued cacao beans like gold and used them as money. Evidence of cacao usage dates back 3,900 years to the Amazon basin near the Andes. And 1,500 years later, it had spread north to Central America and southern Mexico.

The Olmecs and the Mayans believed that the cacao tree was a gift from the gods. They dried and roasted the cacao beans. Then they fermented them with water and hot spices like chili peppers. Chocolate was a thick, frothy hot drink. It was very bitter, not sweet at all.

When the Spaniards conquered the Americas in the 1500s, this hot bitter drink was introduced to Spain. After other countries began exploring the Americas, it gradually spread throughout Europe. The Europeans began to add sugar, cinnamon, and other spices.

In 1828, a Dutch chemist discovered a way to make cocoa powder. He also invented a machine to separate the oil from the beans. Cocoa powder was now easy and inexpensive to make. The first chocolate bar was created in 1847. Milk chocolate was created in 1876. In 1879, a new machine created a smooth chocolate. And that was the beginning of the mass-produced chocolate bars that we enjoy today.

Vocabulary _____

Aztecs: アステカ族　　**Amazon basin:** アマゾン川流域の盆地　　**Andes:** アンデス山脈
Olmecs: オルメカ族　　**Mayans:** マヤ族　　**ferment:** 発酵させる　　**frothy:** 泡立つ
not ~ at all: 全く～ではない　　**Spaniards:** スペイン人　　**the Americas:** アメリカ大陸
gradually: 徐々に　　**throughout:** 全体を通して　　**Dutch:** オランダの
a way to do: ～する方法　　**mass-produced:** 大量生産

POST-READING TASKS

A **Check your answer.**

なぞなぞの答えを確認しましょう。

Even though chocolate has a long history, I wasn't invented until the early 1800s. What am I?

ANSWER: You are _____.

B **Complete the sentences.**

1.～5. の文の空欄に入る最も適切なものを a.～e.から選び、文章を完成させましょう

1. The first usage of cacao _____ to the upper Amazon basin.
2. The Olmecs and Mayans _____.
3. As cacao was introduced to the Europeans, _____.
4. Milk chocolate was created almost 30 years _____.
5. Chocolate bars began to be _____.

    a. after the first chocolate bar was made

    b. fermented the cacao and made a hot bitter drink

    c. mass-produced around the 1880s

    d. goes back almost 6000 years

    e. they began to drink it as a hot sweet drink

C **More on the Topic**

録音を聞いて、（　　）を埋めましょう。

(   ) trees traditionally grow in the shade in the (   ). Its tiny white (   ) grow right on the trunk. They face (   ) and are very intricate. Only one kind of (   ) can get (   ) to pollinate them. That is the chocolate midge, a (   ) you can hardly see. (   ) cacao flowers have over (   ) aroma ingredients, which attract the (   ). Cacao plantations replaced rainforests, but neither the (   ) nor the (   ) thrive on them. The flowers have (   ) aroma ingredients, and only (   ) of every (   ) flowers get pollinated. Now, most cacao is grown on (   ) (   ) (   ) in Africa, but its future is still at stake.

Vocabulary _____

grow right on the trunk:（木の）幹から直接生えてくる　　**intricate:** 複雑な

pollinate: 受粉する　　**chocolate midge:** チョコレートミッジ（極小のハエ）

ingredient: 成分　　**be at stake:** 危機に瀕している

D　**Answer the questions.**

1.～6. の質問の答えを a.～f.から選んで、空欄に記入しましょう

_____ **1.** Where does cacao traditionally grow?

_____ **2.** What do the cacao flowers look like?

_____ **3.** How big are the chocolate midges?

_____ **4.** How do wild cacao flowers differ from those grown on plantations?

_____ **5.** Why are cacao plantations not very successful?

_____ **6.** Where is most cacao now being grown?

    a. Under other trees in the rainforest.

    b. The wild flowers have many more aroma ingredients.

    c. The trees and midges don't thrive, but disease and pests do.

    d. They are small, intricate and face down.

    e. On small family farms in Africa.

    f. They are so small that they are hard to see.

E　**What did you learn from the lesson?**

録音を聴いて（　　）に単語をいれ、ペアになって会話を練習しましょう。

A: How did you enjoy the lesson?

B: Well, I found it (　　　　　). And you?

A: I found it (　　　　　). What did you find (　　　　　)?

B: Well, I was fascinated by cacao's long history, especially in the 1800s. What did you find (　　　　)?

A: Well, I love chocolate. But I hate how we have destroyed the environment in order to grow it

Lesson 11

Keeping Time around the World

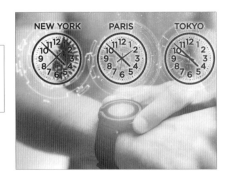

PRE-READING TASKS

Fast Fact

Astronomical time and atomic time are two ways science defines time.

A 次の 1.~3.の文の空欄に入る適切なものを a.~c.から選び、文章を完成させましょう。

1. Atomic time is measured by _____.
2. Astronomical time is measured by _____.
3. One second is 1/60th of a minute in astronomical time, _____ in atomic time.

    a. by counting the number of times an atom vibrates
    b. but its 9,192,631,770 vibrations of a cesium-133 atom
    c. how long it takes the Earth to turn on its axis

B なぞなぞに挑戦してみましょう。

How can you arrive before you leave?

● Take a guess: _____.

● Read the passage to find out the answer!

Vocabulary _____

keep time: 時を刻む   **astronomical:** 天文学的な   **define:** 定義する
vibrate: 振動する   **cesium-133:** セシウム 133   **turn:**（～を中心に）回る   **axis:** 軸

READING

Our days begin when the sun rises and end when it sets. But as people in Tokyo are getting up, people in New York City are going to bed. "Now" is "now" everywhere, but there are many different times.

Each city used to keep its own time. For example, in the 1800s, the US
5 had hundreds of local times. Transportation was very slow, so this did not cause any problems. But that changed with the railroad. With so many local times, the train schedule was very confusing. Even train accidents happened. So, in 1883, the railroad companies created just four time zones for the US.

10 Indeed, not just a national but a worldwide time system was needed. An international meeting was held in 1884 in Washington, DC. First, they divided the world vertically into 360 degrees. Greenwich, England, was 0 degrees longitude. Then they divided those 360 degrees by 24 hours. Each hour was 15 degrees wide.

15 They also made an imaginary line through the Pacific Ocean. They called it the International Date Line. Each date ends there, and a new date begins from there. So, if you go east over the Date Line, you can go back in time. For example, if you fly from Tokyo to Vancouver, you will arrive before you leave.

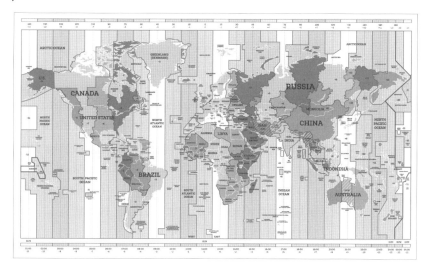

Vocabulary —————————

hold (a meeting): （会議を）開く　　**divide:** 分ける　　**vertically:** 縦に
longitude: 経度　　**imaginary:** 架空の　　**International Date Line:** 国際日付変更線

POST-READING TASKS

A **Check your answer.**

なぞなぞの答えを確認しましょう。

How can you arrive before you leave?

YOUR ANSWER: _____.

B **Complete the sentences.**

1.~5. の文の空欄に入る最も適切なものを a.~e.から選び、文章を完成させましょう

1. As the Earth turns, half of the world is day, _____.
2. Each place used to keep its own time, _____.
3. But that created many problems _____.
4. A meeting held in 1884 _____.
5. The imaginary line where the date changes _____.

    a. goes through the middle of the Pacific Ocean

    b. according to when the sun rose and set

    c. created a new international time system

    d. with the birth of the train

    e. while the other half is night

C **More on the Topic**

録音を聞いて、（　　　）を埋めましょう。

44

Even though there is an international (   ) (   ), it is not international (   ). So each country can (   ) the (   ) (   ) within its own country. If you look at the map of the (   ) (   ), you will not see (   ) vertical lines. In fact, the lines zigzag down the map. For example, the 50 US states, including Alaska and Hawaii, use (   ) time zones. China covers (   ) time zones, but it uses (   ) (   ) for the whole country. So, in the (   ) part of China, the (   ) doesn't (   ) until (   ) a.m. Actually, only the military uses (   ) (   )-degree time zones.

Vocabulary _____

zigzag down: ジグザグに下る   **military:** 軍隊

D Answer the questions.

1.～4. の質問の答えを a.～d.から選んで、空欄に記入しましょう

_____ **1.** Why can countries decide their own time zones?
_____ **2.** How many time zones does the US use?
_____ **3.** How many time zones does China use?
_____ **4.** Who uses 24 equal time zones?

    a. Because there is no international law.
    b. The military.
    c. Half a dozen.
    d. Just one.

E What did you learn from the lesson?

録音を聴いて（　　）に単語をいれ、ペアになって会話を練習しましょう。

A: How did you enjoy the lesson?

B: Well, I found it (　　　　　). And you?

A: I found it (　　　　　). What did you find (　　　　)?

B: Well, we only have one time zone here in Japan. So we never really have to think about different time zones. What about you?

A: Well, I found it (　　　　　). Each country can decide their own system, so it is still so complicated.

Lesson

12

What Would We Do without Glass?

PRE-READING TASKS

Fast Fact

Sand, lime and soda ash, heated till they melt, become glass.

A 次の 1.～3.の文の空欄に入る適切なものを a.～c.から選び、文章を完成させましょう。

1. Obsidian is a kind of natural glass ＿＿＿＿＿＿.
2. Sand hit by a lightning bolt ＿＿＿＿＿＿.
3. Glass is not classified as a solid, ＿＿＿＿＿＿.

    a. because molecules can still move around inside it

    b. formed by volcanic lava that has cooled quickly

    c. may also turn into glass

B なぞなぞに挑戦してみましょう。

I am a type of glass used in almost every modern building, but I wasn't invented until 1000AD. What am I?

● Take a guess: You are ＿＿＿＿＿＿＿＿.

● Read the passage to find out the answer!

Vocabulary ＿＿＿＿＿＿＿

soda ash: ソーダ灰（工業用無水炭酸ナトリウム）　　**obsidian:** 黒曜石　　**classify A as B:** A を B に分類する　　**move around:** 動き回る　　**volcanic :** 火山の　　**lava:** 溶岩

READING

Can you imagine a world without glass? Homes, buildings, cars and trains with no glass windows! No glass bottles and jars to preserve things! No light bulbs! No eyeglasses! But who discovered this amazing material?

Sadly, we will probably never know the earliest history of glassmaking. 5 Glass breaks down over time and simply disappears, especially when it gets wet. The oldest manmade glass objects are beads from about 3500BC. They were found in Egypt and the Near East. Glass vases from 1500 BC were also found there. The ancient glassmakers crushed small quartz rocks and melted them over a fire. They made beautiful blues, reds, purples and 10 other colors by adding various minerals. As valuable as silver, gold and gems, this colorful glass was highly treasured.

Glass-blowing was discovered in Syria in the 1ˢᵗ century BC. It became easier, faster, and cheaper to make glass objects. Now, even common people could afford them. But still, there was no clear glass. That was invented in 15 Alexandria in Egypt about a thousand years later. After that, the Romans became the first to use glass in architecture.

By the 1300s, Venice became the center of glassmaking, and it began to spread throughout Europe. More advances were made over the centuries. But beginning with the Industrial Revolution in the late 1800s, new man-20 ufacturing processes gave us the glass we know today.

Vocabulary _____

bead: ビーズ（手芸に使う小さな玉）　　**quartz:** 石英　　**as A as B:** A と B が同じように
gems: 宝石　　**glass-blowing:** 吹きガラス　　**architecture:** 建築
Industrial Revolution: 産業革命　　**manufacturing process:** 製造法の

POST-READING TASKS

A **Check your answer.**

なぞなぞの答えを確認しましょう。

I am a type of glass used in almost every modern building, but I wasn't invented until 1000AD. What am I?

ANSWER: You are _____.

B **Complete the sentences.**

1.～5. の文の空欄に入る最も適切なものを a.～e.から選び、文章を完成させましょう

1. Glass breaks down rather easily, _____.
2. Small quartz rocks, not sand, _____.
3. Ancient glassmakers knew _____.
4. Common people were able to buy glass objects _____.
5. With the spread of the Roman Empire, _____.

    a. how to make a variety of colors
    b. after glassblowing was invented
    c. so there is no record of the earliest manmade glass
    d. glassmaking spread throughout Europe
    e. was the source of the glass found in Egypt and the Near East

C **More on the Topic**

録音を聞いて、(　　　) を埋めましょう。

After (　　　　) glass was discovered, someone noticed that images (　　　　) convex-shaped glass appeared (　　　　). Convex glass objects were made to place over (　　　　). Later, someone put a couple in front of their (　　　　), and (　　　　) were born! Mostly, monks used glasses when (　　　　) text. (　　　　) them in (　　　　) of the eyes was a problem. Various solutions were tried over the years. Of course, each person's (　　　　) was different, too. (　　　　) glass only helped far-sighted people. Then someone discovered concave glass helped near-sighted people. Glass (　　　　) gradually improved, as well as ways to (　　　　) people's (　　　　). But actually, it has been only a (　　　　) since eyeglasses have become available to (　　　　) people.

Vocabulary _____

convex-shaped: 凸型の   **place over:** 〜の上に置く   **put A in front of B:** A を B の目の前に置く   **monk:** 僧侶   **far-sighted:** 遠視の   **concave:** 凹面の
near-sighted: 近視の   **become available:** 普及する

D **Answer the questions.**

1.〜6. の質問の答えを a.〜f.から選んで、空欄に記入しましょう

_____ **1.** What kind of glass makes things appear larger?
_____ **2.** How were these first objects used?
_____ **3.** When did the monks use them?
_____ **4.** What was a problem with the first eyeglasses?
_____ **5.** What kind of glass helps near-sighted people?
_____ **6.** When did eyeglasses become common?

     a. When they were copying text.
     b. Only about a hundred years ago.
     c. Concave glass.
     d. Convex glass.
     e. They were placed over writing
     f. Keeping them in front of the eyes.

E **What did you learn from the lesson?**

録音を聴いて（   ）に単語をいれ、ペアになって会話を練習しましょう。

A: How did you enjoy the lesson?

B: Well, I found it very (   ). And you?

A: I found it (   ), too. What did you find (   )?

B: Well, I never really thought about all the glass we use. It's everywhere, isn't it?! What about you?

A: Well, I totally agree with you. Plastic has replaced a lot of glass, but glass is still important, isn't it?

Lesson

13 Not Your Usual Building Materials

PRE-READING TASKS

Fast Fact

Growing at about 5cm an hour, bamboo is the fastest-growing plant on Earth.

A 次の 1.～3.の文の空欄に入る適切なものを a.～c.から選び、文章を完成させましょう。

1. Over 1,500 species of bamboo grow _____.
2. Softwood trees are harvested for lumber in 10 to 20 years, _____.
3. Each bamboo clump can produce _____.

   a. but bamboo can be harvested in just three to five years
   b. 200 poles every three to five years
   c. throughout Asia, Australia, the Americas and Sub-Saharan Africa

B なぞなぞに挑戦してみましょう。

I am very hard and strong, and I am used as a support in all modern buildings. But some bamboo is even stronger than I am. That surprised me! What am I?

● Take a guess: You are _____.

● Read the passage to find out the answer!

Vocabulary _____

building material: 建材   **softwood tree:** 針葉樹   **harvest:** 収穫する、伐採する

lumber : 材木   **clump:** 塊   **Sub-Saharan Africa:** アフリカのうちサハラ砂漠より南の地域

READING

Have you ever seen a bamboo house? Probably not. Termites and certain beetles love to eat bamboo, so bamboo is not often used as a building material. But, thanks to the Green School and Ibuku in Bali, that is changing. They created a special natural treatment using
5 boron. After the treatment, insects cannot digest the bamboo.

Now there are many good reasons to build with bamboo. First, bamboo is not only beautiful and flexible, it is as strong as steel! Some species grow as high as 40 meters. Bamboo is extremely friendly to the environment, too. It releases 35 percent more oxygen than other trees.
10 Some species absorb up to 12 tons of carbon dioxide per hectare. On top of that, it grows well on degraded land.

Ibuku builds unbelievably creative and beautiful bamboo structures. They use both modern engineering and the wisdom of Bali's traditional craftsmen. A model is made with bamboo sticks. Then a 3D
15 computer model is created. Architects and engineers study it to make sure it is structurally sound.

The foundations are made with stone, concrete and steel. The rest is all made by hand from bamboo. They are designed to have as little impact on the environment as possible.
20

Vocabulary

termite: 白アリ   **Ibuku:** 竹を建材にしている建築会社   **boron:** ホウ素
extremely: 非常に   **absorb:** 吸い上げる、吸収する   **carbon dioxide:** 二酸化炭素
on top of that : その上   **degraded:** 荒廃した   **craftsmen:** 職人   **model:** 模型
be sound: 健全であること   **as little ~ as possible:** できるだけ～しないように
impact: 影響、衝撃

POST-READING TASKS

A **Check your answer.**

なぞなぞの答えを確認しましょう。

I am very hard and strong, and I am used as a support in all modern build-ings. But some bamboo is even stronger than I am. That surprised me! What am I?

ANSWER: You are _____.

B **Complete the sentences.**

1.～5. の文の空欄に入る最も適切なものを a.～e.から選び、文章を完成させましょう

1. Bamboo has not been used as a building material _____.
2. The special ingredient used in the bamboo treatment _____.
3. Some bamboo species release more oxygen and absorb more carbon dioxide _____.
4. Ibuku's designs bring together _____.
5. Other than the foundation, _____.

    a. both modern and traditional knowledge and wisdom

    b. than most other kinds of trees

    c. is boron

    d. Ibuku's structures are made entirely by hand with bamboo

    e. because insects would eat it

C **More on the Topic**

録音を聞いて、（　　）を埋めましょう。

Another unique (　　　　) (　　　　　) is packed (　　　　　). Most Inuits lived in homes made from (　　　　　) and hides. They would pack (　　　) around them to keep in the (　　　　). Snow has many (　　　) pockets, so it becomes an insulator. Outside it may be -(　　　　　)°C, but inside it ranges from -(　　　　)°C to (　　　　)°C, warmed by (　　　　) heat alone. Actually, the dome-shaped igloos were used only by the Inuit who live up in the far north. They range from (　　　　　) shelters, to single-family homes, to connected structures that can house up to (　　　　) people. A single-family igloo can be built in just a (　　　　) hours.

Vocabulary _____

Inuits : イヌイット　　　**hides:** 皮　　　**insulator:** 断熱材、絶縁体
igloo: イグルー　　　**single-family home:** 一戸建て住宅　　　**house (v):** 住む
up to: 最大〜まで

D　**Answer the questions.**

1.〜5. の質問の答えを a.〜e.から選んで、空欄に記入しましょう

_____ **1.** What are the traditional building materials of most Inuits?

_____ **2.** How did they use the snow?

_____ **3.** Why does snow act as an insulator?

_____ **4.** How much difference might there be between inside and outside temperatures?

_____ **5.** How long does it take to build an igloo?

　　a. A couple hours.

　　b. They packed it around their houses.

　　c. Up to 61°C different.

　　d. Whalebones, hides and snow.

　　e. Because it has many air pockets.

E　**What did you learn from the lesson?**

録音を聴いて（　　）に単語をいれ、ペアになって会話を練習しましょう。

A: How did you enjoy the lesson?

B: Well, I found it (　　　　　). And you?

A: I found it (　　　　　). What did you find (　　　　　)?

B: The beautiful bamboo homes, of course! I'd like to live in a home like that.

A: Yeah, me too. I found it (　　　　　) to see how people use the materials available to them. I never imagined that snow could keep you warm!

Lesson

14 Nuclear Fusion, the Future of Energy

PRE-READING TASKS

Fast Fact

We have three main sources of energy: nuclear, fossil and renewable.

A 次の 1.～3.の文の空欄に入る適切なものを a.～c.から選び、文章を完成させましょう。

1. There are two kinds of nuclear energy, _____, that is, breaking nuclei apart or combining two or more nuclei together.
2. Fossil energy includes _____.
3. Renewable sources include _____..

    a. oil, coal and natural gas

    b. wind power, solar power, geothermal power and hydropower

    c. fission and fusion

B なぞなぞに挑戦してみましょう。

I use nuclear fusion to produce the light and heat you experience on Earth. What am I?

● Take a guess: You are the _____.

● Read the passage to find out the answer!

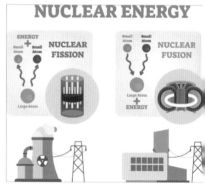

Vocabulary

fusion: 融合   **break ~ apart:** ～に分裂する、分解する   **nuclei:** 核
combine ~ together: ～を結合する   **solar power:** 太陽光発電
geothermal power: 地熱発電   **hydropower:** 水力発電   **fission:** 分裂

READING

54

Did you know there are two kinds of nuclear energy? One is produced by nuclear fission, the other by nuclear fusion. Both reactions produce lots of energy. But the fuels they use and their by-products are completely different.

5   The sun produces energy by nuclear fusion in its core. At extremely high temperatures and high pressure, the nuclei of hydrogen fuse together and become helium. That new helium weighs a little less than the original hydrogen. That lost weight was turned into energy during the reaction. In the sun, over 600 million metric tons of hydrogen fuse together every sec-
10 ond. It is a safe, clean form of energy.

55

On Earth, we have used nuclear fission for the past 70 years. An atom is broken apart to create two or more atoms. Uranium is usually used as fuel. The nuclear reaction produces a great amount of energy. This energy heats water to make steam, which is used to make electricity. However, ra-
15 dioactive waste is also produced. On top of that, devastating accidents have happened. It takes years and lots of money to build and, later, to tear down the plants.

So why aren't we using nuclear fusion, instead? Well, the heat and pressure of the sun's core must be produced on a consistent, stable basis. For
20 years, it took more energy to create such a reaction than the reaction produced. But in just the past 10 years, research and development have come a long way. Research institutes and commercial start-ups are already building and testing various prototypes. Some now predict a commercial model may be ready as early as 2025.

Vocabulary _____

reaction: 反応   **fuel:** 燃料   **by-product:** 副産物   **fuse together:** 融合する
helium: ヘリウム   **metric ton:** メートルトン、1MT=1000kg
uranium: ウラン   **radioactive waste:** 放射性廃棄物   **devastating:** 壊滅的な
consistent: 一貫性のある   **stable:** 安定した   **come a long way:** 大きな発展を遂げる
research institute: 研究機関   **start-ups:** 新興企業、新規事業   **prototypes:** 試作品
predict: 予測する

POST-READING TASKS

A **Check your answer.**

なぞなぞの答えを確認しましょう。

I use fusion to produce the light and heat you experience on Earth. What am I?

ANSWER: You are the _____.

B **Complete the sentences.**

1.～5. の文の空欄に入る最も適切なものを a.～e.から選び、文章を完成させましょう

1. While fusion and fission are both nuclear reactions, _____.
2. When hydrogen fuses together during nuclear fusion _____.
3. When a uranium atom is broken apart during nuclear fission, _____.
4. Nuclear fusion has not been used as an energy resource up till now _____.
5. Recently, research and development have progressed rapidly, _____.

    a. because scientists could not produce the necessary conditions
    b. energy and radioactive waste are produced
    c. energy and helium are produced
    d. and a nuclear fusion reactor are no longer a dream
    e. their fuels and by-products are different

C **More on the Topic**

録音を聞いて、（ ）を埋めましょう。

Imagine a ( ) ( ) ( ). First, it takes up lots of ( ). The ( ) and cooling towers are imposing and ( ). Radioactive fuels and wastes are stored there. Very strict security measures are needed. Now imagine a ( ) ( ). ( ) reactors are about that size. Each will be able to create enough energy for ( ) homes. One company uses ( ) and ( ) as fuel. They are ( ), abundant and do not need to be mined. No carbon or ( ) byproducts are produced. If a reaction fails, ( ) happens, so it's not ( ). In the near future, small nuclear fusion plants may be built right in our communities.

Vocabulary _____

take up: 場所を取る   **cooling tower:** 冷却塔   **imposing:** 人目を引く
store: 貯蔵する   **security measure:** 安全対策   **abundant:** 豊富な   **mine (v):** 採掘する

D **Answer the questions.**

1.～5. の質問の答えを a.～e. から選んで、空欄に記入しましょう

_____ **1.** What are big, imposing and ugly?
_____ **2.** What is one demerit of nuclear fission?
_____ **3.** How big is a nuclear fusion reactor?
_____ **4.** What is one merit of hydrogen and boron?
_____ **5.** What happens if a nuclear fusion reaction fails?

    a. It's about the size of a tennis court.
    b. The buildings and cooling towers of nuclear power plants are.
    c. It produces radioactive waste.
    d. Nothing, therefore it is very safe.
    e. They are cheap.

E **What did you learn from the lesson?**

録音を聴いて（　　）に単語をいれ、ペアになって会話を練習しましょう。

A: How did you enjoy the lesson?

B: Well, I found it (　　　　　). And you?

A: I found it (　　　　　). What did you find (　　　　　)?

B: Well, I thought all nuclear energy was very dangerous. Nuclear fusion is just the opposite!

A: Right. I hope nuclear fusion will help to make a better, cleaner world for everyone.

身近な不思議の世界

検印
省略

© 2023年1月31日　初版発行

著　者　　　　　　　　　　　Mary Tadokoro

発行者　　　　　　　　　　　小川　洋一郎

発行所　　　　　　　　　株式会社　朝日出版社
101-0065　東京都千代田区西神田 3-3-5
電話　東京 (03) 3239-0271/72
FAX　東京 (03) 3239-0479
e-mail　text-e@asahipress.com
振替口座　00140-2-46008
組版／クロス・コンサルティング　製版／錦明印刷

乱丁・落丁はお取り替えいたします。
ISBN978-4-255-15701-6　C1082